DEATH'S DOOR

The Pursuit of a Legend

Conan Bryant Eaton

Published 1967
Revised edition 1974
Third edition, revised 1980, Second printing 1987
Fourth edition 1996

Published by Jackson Harbor Press
RR1, Box 107AA
Washington Island, WI 54246

Printed in USA

Publisher's Cataloging-in-Publication Data
Eaton, Conan Bryant, 1909-1991
Death's Door, The Pursuit of a Legend/by Conan
    Bryant Eaton; with illustrations by Katie West
Summary: Legends and facts about the naming of
    Death's Door in Door County, Wisconsin
            1. Door County, WI -- Death's Door   2. Maritime -
            history of Death's Door, Wisconsin
I. West, Katie, ill.
II. Title
977.5

Library of Congress Catalog Card Number
96-76172

ISBN 0-9640210-7-2

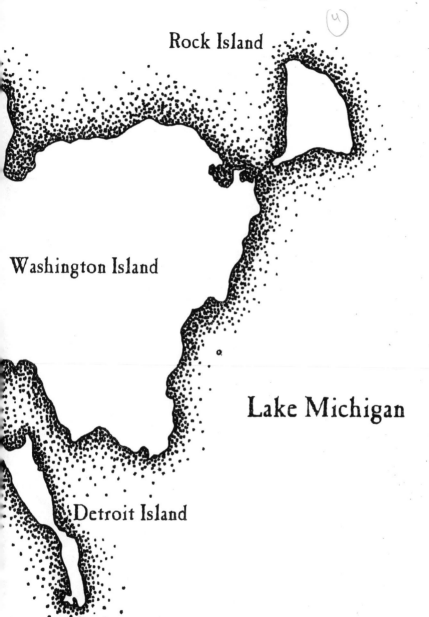

Rock Island

Washington Island

Lake Michigan

Detroit Island

⊗
ilot Island

* Lighthouses

This edition of Death's Door is gratefully dedicated to
Eelin and Steve Eaton.

FOREWORD

Conan Bryant Eaton, a long-time resident of Washington Island, Wisconsin, published *Death's Door: The Pursuit of A Legend* in 1967. Because this work continues to be the most authoritative writing ever done on the hazardous Death's Door passage, we believe it richly merits re-publication.

Death's Door is one of four booklets Conan issued in his "Island Series," as he put it, "a part of the history of Washington Township." His theme engages our attention for several reasons: marine disasters fascinate us all because they represent a life-and-death struggle for survival against the mighty forces of nature. Those of us who love the sea, love also ships and lighthouses, pounding surf and gale-force winds. . . and tales of tragedy and heroism. Of such is this book.

Buried in the mists of time, the legend of Death's Door is part truth and part fiction, part history and part imagination. The watery passage from which Door County receives its name continues to this day to challenge the mettle of seafarers, especially in the autumn of each year.

Conan's last words on this intriguing subject appeared in 1974: "Practically all known marine disasters laid at Death's Door have been suffered in attempting to pass *through* the strait (chiefly in the days of sailing ships), while most local hardships and losses -- and even the well-known legend itself -- are concerned with attempts to *cross* the notorious passage. And although the Door's threat has gradually diminshed in the wake of technological progress, these waters still work their influence on daily life in this vicinity. Those who live upon -- and those who visit -- the islands of the Town of Washington can hardly be unaware even today of timeless Porte des Morts' disturbing presence."

As Conan did before us, "We frequently make cuts in quoted material, indicating them with dots... But we treasure the original writer's meaning, as we do his spelling, grammar, punctuation and capitalization, which stand unchanged. Within the limits of typography available to us, we retain the antique appearance of old writings such as Hennepin's and Carver's, believing that to modernize them would be to put modern overalls on Hamlet's grave-diggers.

"The frequently-quoted sources which we abbreviate in the footnotes are these:

"The State Historical Society of Wisconsin Collections (Madison); cited as *WHC*.

"The briefs of both states in the action *In the Supreme Court of the United States, October Term, 1925, Original No. 19 -- In Equity;* cited as *Wisbrief* and *Michbrief.*

"We took comfort in the help and courtesies of friends and institutions, and take pleasure in thanking them. We are grateful to:

"The libraries of Washington Island, Door County, Green Bay, Milwaukee, the State Historical Society of Wisconsin, Loretto Convent in Sault Sainte Marie, Michigan, The Newberry Library of Chicago; also Jacobsen's Museum of Washington Island.

"William G. Haygood and Paul Vanderbilt of Madison; Dr. Helene Monod-Cassidy (Mrs. Fred Cassidy) of Madison and Washington Island; Mrs. Alvin Cornell, Ray Krause, the Mac Magnussons, Charlotte Meyer, the Arni Richters, Angus Swenson and Wilson Trueblood of Washington Island; Sister Alice and Father Robert Prud'homme of Sault Sainte Marie, Michigan; Chief Roy Oshkosh of Egg Harbor; Adolph Schinkten, and the staff of the *Door County Advocate*, Sturgeon Bay."

"This amateur historian," Conan continues, "confesses to occasional envy of writers of an earlier day, when prevailing literary styles permitted a candor which is out of fashion today. We should like to say as A.C. Wheeler did in his 1861 *Chronicles of Milwaukee*:

'In presenting this book ... the Author asks no indulgence; his object, he must be permitted to say is a good one, and those who do not admire the execution have the same privilege to grumble that he had to write.' "

We are especially indebted to Katie West for providing us with the excellent illustrations which appear in this, the 1996 edition of this work, and to Jackson Harbor Press for assistance given.

Goodwin Berquist, Chairman
Kathy Findlay
Sylvia Nelson
Bill Olson
Rhea Sikes

Eaton Book Committee
Town of Washington
Historical Archives Committee

DEATH's DOOR
The Pursuit of a Legend

Legends of Michigan and the Old North West confesses that its stories about Indians are "gleaned along the uncertain, misty line, dividing traditional from historic times."[1] This is the misty line we must approach if we hope to find the beginnings of a legend which has surely been told for one hundred fifty years and perhaps much longer.

The Death's Door name derives, we are often told, from an ancient Indian legend. This we may at least tentatively accept, considering the testimony of many years, and the definition of "legend" as "Any story coming down from the past, especially one popularly taken as historical though not verifiable."[2] Surely it seems possible that Indians of this region may have passed the germ of today's Death's Door legend from one generation to another, for we know that "...Our Wisconsin tribesmen had stories, myths, and legends about many of the springs, streams, lakes, prairies, woodlands, rocks, hills, and valleys of the regions, which were theirs...In the centuries of their occupation of their homeland, as a result of their life experiences and culture, a wealth of tales and legends became attached to many of the scenic landmarks of their environment."[3]

But we should be cautious in accepting these tales as history, for "... the Indians have a peculiar habit of 'continued stories,' by which at the tepee fire one will take up some well known tale and add to it and so make a new story of it, or at least a new conclusion. As with the minstrels and minnesingers of feudal Europe at the tournaments, the best fellow is the one who tells the most thrilling tale."[4]

Lest we look too smugly on the "peculiar habit" of Indian storytellers, let us remember that it was certain European - not Indian - historians whom John Gilmary Shea called "that amiable class who seem to tell truth by accident and fiction by inclination."[5] We shall have the chance to judge many varying versions of the Death's Door story; perhaps our judgment may gain charity if we consider these words from a United States Supreme Court decision:

"No human transactions are unaffected by time. Its influence is seen on all things subject to change. And this is peculiarly the case in regard to matters which rest in memory, and which consequently fade with the lapse of time, and fall with the lives of individuals."[6]

We deal here with a legend which demonstrably has endured at least a century and a half of telling and re-telling, twisting, shaping, augmenting and embroidering. We gather and examine the recountings of the past, and observe the remarkable workings of human purpose and human memory

2

in transmitting the story of what may have been, at some precise point in history, a very simple occurrence. Finally, we search for the truth about that occurrence.

Unlike the shadowy legend, Death's Door itself is utterly substantial - as real as pounding surf or piles of limestone one hundred feet high, as real as restless waters twenty fathoms deep or icy acres bridging uneasily the surge of hidden currents.

Wholly apart from the legend, the strait has earned a legendary reputation. The very name of the passage seems to make events near it more news-worthy, seems to invite overstatement. Thus, occasional writers cannot resist the temptation to sink La Salle's *Griffin* in Death's Door, improbable as that fate may be.[7] There is no doubt that September of 1679 saw the first well-recorded crossing in a storm of the turbulent strait. The *Griffin* had sailed, the Recollect friar Hennepin tells us, from the "Ifland juft at the Mouth of the Bay," and a day later LaSalle's party of fourteen departed in "four Canoùs...laden with a Smith's Forge, and Inftruments, and Tools for Carpenters, Joyners, and Sawyers, befides our Goods and Arms. We fteer'd to the South towards the Continent...about the middle of the way, in the Night-time, we were furpriz'd with a fudden Storm, whereby we were in great danger. The waves came into our Canoùs; and the night was fo dark, that we had much ado to keep company together; However, we got afhoar the next day..."[8]

The dangers besetting La Salle have not lessened in three hundred years. Two official sources describe them this way:

"Porte des Morts (Death's Door) passage. - There is a strong current setting in or out according to the direction of the wind, and many vessels have been lost in consequence; it is frequently so strong that sailing vessels can not make headway against it. The coast is rock bound and certain destruction awaits the craft going ashore. Sometimes the current is against the wind."[9]

"Porte des Morts Passage, Wis...is known as 'Death's Door,' owing to the numerous detached reefs and shoals obstructing its navigation...almost certain destruction to craft going ashore. These conditions have been the cause of many vessel disasters."[10]

Any list of losses in and around Death's Door rings with a mournful music like bellbuoys near fog-shrouded shoals.[11] Our search for the legend will make us witnesses to some events in the passage, but there are many thrilling stories which have no connection with the legend:

"In November, 1853, in an old lumber brig...We left Chicago under full sail with a brisk south wind, and early the second night out, were at Port Du Mort's or Death's Door. In the act of coming up to the wind to enter the Door we were met by a gale of wind from the northwest. The old brig failed to come in stays and the captain was obliged to wear ship and in doing so we passed out within twenty five feet of the Door Bluffs, reaching the open lake where we scudded under bare poles until we were abreast of Milwaukee when the wind abated sufficiently to enable the Captain to again make sail and head her again for Green Bay."[12]

The Fredericksons of Frankfort, Michigan raised in the atmosphere of Great Lakes navigation recount that:

"On Sept. 26, 1888, the heavily laden schooner *Fleetwing*...was making ready for another trip...Dusk was approaching...her sails were set for the trip across the bay...with an increasing westerly wind she made good way...the captain shaped his course and hoped for a fast trip through the dreaded Death's Door Passage and on into the waters of the big lake. In the early days of sail it required a lot of luck and first class seamanship to make the passage after dark or in periods of poor visibility... The *Fleetwing* ...soon fetched the dark shadows of the high land close aboard on her starboard bow. In the darkness the captain mistakenly took Death's Door Bluff for Table Bluff and dropped her off to the eastward for a passage through the narrows of the Door...After running a short time on this heading the captain became alarmed at seeing no welcoming loom of an opening in the darkness or the lights of Plum and Pilot Islands up ahead and ordered the helm 'hard down' and commanded the watch to 'about ship'...she ran out of sea room and fetched up standing, with a terrible splintering crash, on the rocky beach...When the storm was over...the ship had almost gone to pieces where she lay."[13]

Even when used in a humorous account, the Death's Door name retains its character as a symbol of marine oblivion. An 1861 history suggests that, had certain Milwaukeeans known the problems involved when they purloined a steamboat from Buffalo, "they might have *left her in the Porte du Morte*."[14]

A *Pictorial Marine History* published in Sturgeon Bay tells us:

"A diary of the lighthouse keeper of Plum Island, kept from 1872 to 1889,[15] indicates that winds and roaring seas with a shipwreck at least twice a week was the usual course of things. In the fall of 1872 eight large vessels stranded or shipwrecked in 'Death's Door'...in one week ...in 1872, almost a hundred vessels were lost or seriously damaged passing through the 'Door'...The worst storm that ever occurred on Lake Michigan up to 1880, came out of the south on October 15 of that year (the Alpena Gale)[16]...In the vicinity of Plum Island, in Death's Door, there was in the neighborhood of thirty vessels driven ashore."

5

"The schooner *Resumption*, one of the few large sailing vessels on the Great Lakes in the nineteen hundreds, found its final resting place November 7, 1914, on Plum Island, Death's Door passage...bound from Chicago to Wells, Mich., in light trim, with a heavy gale blowing from the southwest. On reaching the Door she attempted to come about when abreast of Plum Island, but missed stays and before the anchor could be lowered she had been carried up on the beach by the wind and sea...she was abandoned as a total wreck..." This shipwreck is a boyhood memory of Washington Island's Milton Cornell, whose father was first assistant lighthouse keeper on Pilot at the time. "We watched her from the tower," says Milton, "and went aboard the next day." He recalls the crew's hands, burned from letting down the sails so fast in the emergency. [17]

The heyday of sail undoubtedly saw the greatest concentration of wreckage in Death's Door passage. During most of this period at least one beacon shone for the guidance of mariners; we can only guess what terrors the waterway held for sailing vessels before it was lighted. Happily, in those earlier days the ships with business in Green Bay were few, and the wider Rock Island passage (lighted from 1837 on) attracted most of them.

But increasing commerce between southern Lake Michigan and the port of Green Bay made the shorter Death's Door passage a near-necessity. In 1837 Lt. Pendergast, having surveyed the Great Lakes to determine where lighthouses were most needed, reported to the Board of Navy Commissioners: "Entrance of Green Bay--...The south or Port de Mort passage... is without a light, and I beg leave to strongly recommend that one be placed there as soon as convenient. It should be a colored light..."[18]

1848 arrived before Congress appropriated $3500 for construction of a light in Death's Door. It was built and put into operation, apparently, for $3125.80![19] The possible existence of a light on Plum Island before 1836 has been suggested, but remains unproven.[20] In 1850 a lighthouse was established on Pilot Island, and by 1858 the Plum Island beacon was discontinued. Almost forty years passed before the Government, in 1896, built a new Plum Island light. Meanwhile, tiny Pilot stood as the only guide for shipping through Death's Door.[21]

7

The increase of precisely controllable power gradually put into sailors' hands the ability to resist those natural forces which still move unhindered in the strait. Electronic depth-finding, range-finding and communications aids have removed the sting of Death's Door. But even the most self-assured human must look on with awe when the waterway occasionally shows its fiercest face.

"After taking on a load of sand at Green Island... the sandsucker *Sinaloa*, got caught in the southwest gale that swept over the greater portion of the Great Lakes on November 12, 1940. When in Death's Door...the big steamer got caught in a cross sea, from which the terrific rolling caused the steam lines to break, steering gear became disabled, dynamos were put out of business, and in darkness the steamer drifted across the north end of Green Bay, going on the beach at Sac bay...Big Bay de Noc, Michigan."[22]

Seldom does individual man take up unaided the ancient challenge of the Porte des Morts. In the winter of 1846-47 one Charlie Ticknor, weary of getting out staves in the deep snow of Washington Island's woods, and homesick for Illinois, headed south across the Door's ice; he froze to death just short of Fish Creek. Jesse Miner called this "the first Death we have any record of in . . . crossing Death's Door."[23]

The "hardest trip" of well-known early mail carrier Henry Miner, across the Door's ice and to Green Bay and back, was endured in early 1856. In 1865, Patsy Flannigan and Joseph Folwell, hauling the mail between Ephraim and the Island, were marooned by drifting ice in the Door and subsisted three days eating basswood buds on "Plumb" Island. In March, 1866, luck ran out for the mail carrier. Martin (Ole) Oleson disappeared between Eagle Harbor and the Island. Jesse Miner said Ole was "the only mail carrier drowned carrying the mail," and Ole's sack "the only mail-Bag ever lost."

A young lady school teacher dared the ice crossing in 1876, though she prudently followed her parents' orders to travel only with mail carrier Henry Miner.[24] In the same year, the possibility of a tunnel connecting Washington Island with the mainland was being seriously considered on both sides of the Door.[25] And once in the late 1870's there was "no winter at all - no one crossed the Door on the ice all winter." But crossings were made, not only by the mail carrier, but by at least one party which transported three men, a pony and a box of tame rabbits - all in an open pound boat.[26]

One of the period's most harrowing battles with the Door - called in the *Advocate* "A Terrible Night" - was waged by mail carrier Jesse Miner and town treasurer Arni Gudmundsen in March, 1880.[27] Three weeks later, after reporting another "agonizing" trip across the vicious water, the paper's Island correspondent (who had referred to the passage three years earlier as the "blarsted gulf"), complained: "The Door has been simply abominable this winter." Surprisingly, an occasional good word was said for the strait. The *Advocate* in 1884 quoted Rock Island lightkeeper William Betts (who had driven his "ponies" to the county seat) as reporting "the crystal bridge across the Door in a prime condition...the best he has ever seen it."[28]

"So far as is known...the only instance in which a lady has ever crossed the Door alone" was the *Advocate* "s notice of the lonely ten-mile trudge on snowshoes (half the trip after dark) in February, 1885 by Miss Josie Weborg, "preceptress" of Washington Harbor school, who was determined to take advantage of a week's vacation.[29] But as late as January, 1889, when two Island young ladies crossed with mail carrier Cornell, it was still considered

10

"something unusual that 2 young girls would venture"; (Diary of Lincoln Severs, privately owned in Sturgeon Bay).

Between 1885 and 1899, the Island's doctor was frequently ferried across Death's Door in a small row boat or skiff to treat patients on the county's northern mainland.[30]

It appears that the Door has been challenged by an occasional swimmer. A recent example. On September 14, 1973, the Island's Dan and Jens Hansen swam nonstop from the southwest point of Washington Island to the mainland - a distance well over double the actual width of Death's Door itself.

The land-bound or gasoline-powered observer may squint admiringly at the occasional small sailboat making the passage on a sparkling summer day; he will rarely see such a run attempted in questionable weather. Crossing the strait in a vessel even more fragile has become, since the 1800's, so rare it is noteworthy. When in 1958 a Milwaukeean paddled an Eskimo-style kayak from Gills Rock to Detroit Harbor the *Door County Advocate* paid tribute with a news item and a picture three columns wide.[31]

Even today, man does not always win. The people of Washington Island will not forget March 10, 1935, when six young men returning home by automobile from a basketball game on the mainland were betrayed by weakening ice and plunged to death in Death's Door.[32] In October, 1925, the border dispute between Michigan and Wisconsin caused the chambers of the U. S. Supreme Court to echo with the name of Death's Door. Crucial to the Court's decision was the location in 1836 of "*the center of the most usual ship channel*"[33] connecting Green Bay with Lake Michigan. Had Michigan won, the boundary between the two states would have run through Death's Door, and Detroit, Pilot, Plum, Rock and Washington Islands would lie in Michigan.

Wisconsin was upheld, and within her territory still lies the passage in which danger was for so long a reality, and to which legend has clung for a time we have not yet measured.

The Death's Door legend in the modern form which usually confronts us is not difficult to trace. The sources of most of its details and of its dissemination to the general public are clearly two, dating from the years of World War I.[34] From these two tales descend most of the mentions in newspaper and magazine feature stories, the capsule references in tourist oriented advertising, and most other verbal and printed versions of the Death's Door drama from 1917 to the present moment.

And indeed the legend is still with us, a vigorous perennial in Wisconsin's historical and commercial literature. Late in 1966, a handsome national magazine mentioned "Death's Door Bluff, where hundreds of Indians were dashed to death against the rocks in their canoes..."[35] In August of 1965, Door County's *Door Reminder*, a newspaper published in Ellison Bay, printed a short version of the story. And during the winter of 1965-66 Washington Island High School's monthly *Pageant* printed a historical series which included a full-dress recital of the legend.

In 1962 a book titled *Wisconsin Lore*[36] recounted the Death's Door legend at full length. A 1961 tourist guide[37] gives a very brief account, with an interesting variation reversing the Potawatomi's direction of travel. In 1960 the *Chicago Sunday Tribune* Traveler's Guide section said of Death's Door "...the name is said to have originated around 1640 when 300 Potawatomi Indians lost their lives in the strait."[38] Three more sentences saw the Potawatomi to their wretched extinction. And in about 1960 the Door County Chamber of Commerce offered tourists a *Family Fun Map* which included a short version of the aboriginal tragedy. The Washington Island Ferry Line schedule of 1959 gave the story briefly, as did the Island Tourist Bureau folder of 1951.

The early Atomic Age years and even the hectic days of World War II saw the legend far from neglected. Around 1948, Dorothy Moulding Brown published *Wisconsin Indian Place-Name Legends,*[39] repeating a 1915 version verbatim. In 1946, a weighty history of our state referred to Washington Island solely as "Death's Door Island," and seemed to accept the legend with one hundred natives drowned as factual history.[40] Two years before, in his *Old World Wisconsin,* the editor of the above history devoted an excellent chapter to Washington Island, gave a short account of the story with three hundred tribesmen lost, and called the Door "Porte des Mortz."[41]

Critical glances at the legend's varying versions have been nearly non-existent; 1944 is notable for one, from a respected source, The well known historian, editor and onetime Secretary of the State Historical Society of Wisconsin, Milo M. Quaife, in writing in his *Lake Michigan* about "Death Door" cites "An ancient tradition... that here a band of Potawatomi warriors perished while engaged in a foray against their Winnebago enemies." But he adds, "Perhaps a better explanation of the grim name might be found in the disasters which have overtaken mariners since the advent of the first white explorers."[42]

The years of Depression showed a lively interest in the Death's Door legend. The dramatic poem *The Legend of the Door* by Island historian Jens Jacobsen, former Town Chairman, and builder of Jacobsen's Museum, appeared in 1937.[43] And in the 30's another Islander, Eugene Harold Gunnlaugsson, produced a work of the same title which we have seen only in manuscript, but hope to see in print. A climactic stanza tells "The Capture of The Spies":

The spies thus went into enemy land,
To build the fires where there was sand,
So that their friends might safely land,
But, ah, they were caught by the enemy band
Who with a sudden rising ire
Roasted them over a red hot fire.

In the mid-thirties a 1915 version of the legend was included word-for-word in *Wisconsin Indian Place Legends.*[44] A 1934 newspaper feature article[45] adds little flourishes to familiar matter; for example: "... a great storm sent every canoe to the bottom" - a fate we question in the case of birch bark vessels, notwithstanding *A Pictorial Map of Wisconsin* of 1931, which summarizes the legend, and shows Indians and canoes submerging in Death's Door.[46]

In 1929, Agnes Repplier in *Pere Marquette* not only confused Green Bay with Death's Door strait, but attributed the "Porte de la Morte" name merely to "the high winds and roughened waters which had overturned many canoes and drowned many traders."[47]

The sober *Wisconsin Archeologist* in 1920 printed Publius V. Lawson's study of "The Potawatomi" in which he repeated a 1915 version with minor excisions.[48] In 1918 the same periodical printed one of the numerous collateral legends which, while they have no direct connection with the legend of Death's Door, often have a hauntingly suggestive sound:

"A legend concerning this locality states that about two hundred or more years ago six canoe loads of Indians went on a cranberry picking expedition to Manitou Island. They became lost in a fog and drifted across Lake Michigan. When near the shore they heard the waves dash against the rocks at White Fish Bay Point. They landed in safety and

14

named this place Ah qua she ma ganing, meaning 'save our lives'."[49]

This tale is attributed to an interview with Simon Kahquados, identified as "speaker of the Wisconsin band of Pottawatomi at Camp 8, near Wausaukee." To the pursuer of facts about the Death's Door legend, it is thought-provoking that this Potawatomi spokesman, in giving the native names for a number of sites in Door County, fails to mention the Porte des Morts strait under any name, or to make any reference to the legend's existence among his tribesmen. And it makes the searcher's task no simpler when Kahquados relates that "Egg Harbor was called Che bah ye sho da ning, or 'ghost door'."

In 1820, traveling with the Cass expedition along the east shore of Lake Michigan, Captain David Bates Douglass wrote in his journal on September 7: "Fifty canoes of Indians said to have been lost long since on passing from the main to Great Manitou Island-none escaped. They have a superstitious fear of that island ever since."[50] The Manitou Islands are separated from Death's Door by Lake Michigan's full breadth; but the concept of "superstitious fear" is echoed years later in treatments of the Death's Door legend, notably in 1881 (Charles I. Martin's *History of Northern Wisconsin*) and 1917 (Holand's *Door County*).

Henry Rowe Schoolcraft (who was in the 1820 party with Douglass) later gave an Indian account of conflict between Wyandots and Senecas in about 1680, including a canoe battle on Lake Erie in which "the carnage was dreadful."[51] Schoolcraft calls this encounter "somewhat remarkable, as no other tradition makes mention of an Indian battle upon water." Some elements in this account resemble later Death's Door stories.

On September 10, 1863, Door County's *Advocate* reprinted from the *Manitowoc Tribune* an account by one "Alpha" describing a cruise of Door County exploration in

15

the sailing vessel SEA BIRD. The writer says of Death's Door: "This passage...derives its singular cognomen from the historical fact that many years ago some eighty canoe loads of Indians were drowned in its waters by a sudden squall, thus annihilating a whole tribe of aborigines."

On December 4, 1879, the *Advocate* carried a long column concerning the Door and its vicinity, written by an easterner who had visited Pilot Island on business. From local sources or from earlier writings, he gathered this version of the legend: "Nearly the whole tribe of Pottawatamie Indians were drowned while attempting to cross this passage, and the French called it Port du Mort." The visitor may have been prepared to accept any story of the strait's dangers; weather had detained him two weeks in getting out to the island, delayed his departure ten days, even then nearly swamped his boat in the breakers.

A legend version attributed to Islander Ralph Jacobsen offered a "blood curdling close range battle" involving hundreds of Indian-filled canoes during a severe storm, while "poison-stained arrows darkened the sky";. the carnage, it was said, "saved Washington Island for the friendly Potawatomies."[52]

Concerning the earliest version we have found of the Death's Door name, Harvard College Library's Curator of Maps, Dr. Frank E. Trout, was unable in 1967 to find any French map ante-dating 1800 which referred to a headland near the strait between Lake Michigan and Green Bay as "Cap a la Mort" or any variant. He acknowledged the possibility, however, that some early map using such a name might have eluded him.

Two examples of Porte des Morts' continuing power to inspire creators of fiction: The very real tragedy mentioned on page 11 of this booklet was woven by mystery writer, Robert McNear, into his award-winning story "Death's Door," which appeared in *Playboy* in 1969,

16

and was reprinted May, 1971 in *Ellery Queen's Mystery Magazine.*

Even the ubiquitous Paul Bunyan has been dragged into the Death's Door region. Islander Jens Jacobsen recalled (in unpublished reminiscences written about 1947) having heard that when logging in the late 1880s left the Island studded with pine stumps. Several unsuccessful attempts were made to get Paul's blue ox Babe to the Island to pull them out; but the beast, it was said, could not squeeze through the Door.

We have looked backward a full half-century; now we meet the Death's Door legend in its best-known, most-often-borrowed version. Hjalmar Rued Holand's *History of Door County, Wisconsin: The County Beautiful* is the largest, most complete history of the county available; still handy for reference on many Door County shelves and reinforced by the legend's repetition in Holand's smaller *Old Peninsula Days*, it forms the strongest link in the chain connecting the legend's past with the present.[53] Boiled down to essentials, his version amounts to this:

"When the vicious Winnebagos came to the Door County peninsula, they found it occupied by the generous Potawatomi who offered to share the land. The Winnebagos refused, and attacked the less-numerous Potawatomi at every chance. The abused minority withdrew to the nearby islands, but even here faced the threat of invasion by the Winnebagos. The islanders planned a surprise counter-attack across the water, and sent three spies ahead to kindle a beacon to guide their canoes to a safe landing.

"The spies were caught. Under torture one finally told their secret plans. The Winnebagos lit a fire one dark and windy night on a steep bluff which offered only danger.

Meanwhile, they dispatched a canoe detachment by a roundabout route to attack the islanders' camp.

"As the misdirected Potawatomi urged their canoes toward the fire, a great increase in wind and waves cut off all choice of turning back. Their frail craft were broken against the rocky bluff. Some braves drowned, the rest were soon tomahawked by the waiting enemy.

"For their part, the Winnebagos in canoes all were swamped by the seas, and all drowned in the passage. Their tribesmen watched at land's end a full day until finally the wrecked canoes washed up on the shore. They took this loss as an omen that they must never again try to cross the 'Door of Death,' as it was afterward called."

When told in Holand's own words and at its full length, his version is certainly the most thrilling Death's Door legend we have encountered. Indeed, the plethora of thunder and blood presented, plus the wealth of small detail, pique our interest concerning the sources upon which Holand drew. The chapter containing the legend is headed: "Historical Traditions of the Indian Tribes of the Door County Peninsula," and at chapter's end he says: "It would be more correct to call it history in practically all respects except definite dates." A footnote following the legend tells us "This tradition was received by the early fishermen who settled on the islands about 1840 from the Indians who lived there. It is also mentioned by several early travelers. (See Storrow and Stambaugh.)" We shall see these two in their proper time. The very interesting reference in the same note to "Captain Brink" will be examined when we reach 1834.

From his preface we learn that Holand was very familiar with a book of 1881 which contains a legend version; we shall get to it. But let us note here Holand's treatment of some material by George R. Fox, the 1915 writer who told a full-length Death's Door legend. Holand quotes at twelve-page length from Fox's article on signs of

Indian occupation of the islands,[54] but excises neatly Fox's tale of the Indian disaster in Death's Door, referring the reader to his own much lustier version a few pages farther on, (described by Milo M. Quaife as "garnished with modern trimmings").[55] After some examination of Indian legends in general, one feels that Holand's Death's Door story may possibly approximate the characteristics which a genuine Indian legend would show, had it been transmitted to us in an unbroken oral line, uncolored by European contacts. But everything considered, Holand's legend (like several others) seems clearly to be a white man's fiction story about Indians, comparable perhaps to a full-hour television drama expanded from the anecdote about Washington and the cherry tree. We must look back some two hundred years more if we hope to learn more surely whether Holand's tale is history or merely *his story*.

A full recital of George R. Fox's 1915 version begins with his remarks concerning graves found on Detroit Island:

"The supposition is that in this field were buried some of the victims told of in the legend of Death's Door, the passage between Washington Island and the end of Door county.

"As a search through the publications of the Wisconsin Historical Society failed to reveal any mention of this bit of Indian history, it is given in full. It happened before the coming of the French, for by them the official designation of the passage as found on government charts, Porte des Morts (Death's Door), was applied.

"In peace and plenty the Nocquets (?) had long lived on the shores of the islands of the Pottawatomie chain. Hunger they knew not; the lake was full of fish; in the woods were an abundance of deer, bear, turkeys and pigeons, and flocks of ducks and geese frequented the lake and bays. Of all the Islands, Washington was the great game preserve. Never did the great forests on its back refuse food to the hungry man. Hence one day, when a band of Pottawatomies (?), who resided on the neighboring point of Door county, invaded the land of the Nocquets while the latter were away, the Spirit of Trouble spread his mantle over the peaceful isles.

"Though the Indian wanted a deed to the land, though he held no abstract purporting to show how it had passed from hand to hand down from the original grantor, never-the-less his rage was quite as great if not greater than would be that of his white brother when he found some one calmly appropriating to his own use the house he called his own.

"The injury and insult must be wiped out. Fortunately or unfortunately, he had neglected to provide courts and lawyers. The poor redskin had recourse only to bloodshed. War was declared by the simple process of the Nocquet warriors embarking in canoes for a raid on the Pottawatomies. But the medicine men were failures or the braves neglected, in their haste, to propitiate the manido, for they had only gone a portion of the four miles which separated them from their enemies, when a breath of wind struck them, the forerunner of a hurricane which swept the water in green masses over the frail craft.

"Of all the brave band which went forth, not again was one seen alive. To the wives, the mothers, the fathers waiting on the shore, no word came back. Day by day they gazed out over the strait. And then - their warriors came home to them. Tossed up on the beach of Detroit island, friend and relative could do no more than hurry the bodies to hastily prepared graves. Here, in this open space, so the story goes, they were interred."[56]

A little later Fox tells us that "Pictograph rocks are mentioned...as having existed on the rocky bluff near Death's Door."

One interesting detail is Fox's tentative placing of the tribes, making the Potawatomi the interlopers and the Nocquet the injured and revenge-seeking party which took to canoes. (In Hollywood terms, Fox gives Nocquets the white hats and Potawatomi the black.) Another important point is the destruction of the canoe-borne raiders solely by

21

the "hurricane," with no sanguinary contact between the tribes.

Because Fox does not identify his source of the legend, we are permitted conjecture. For the moment let us reveal only that clues exist which hint that he draws upon one or both of two accounts published in 1881.

In one sentence a Green Bay historian of 1913 disposed of the legend: "One of the disasters of these days of Indian occupation is commemorated in the name of 'Death's Door;' a large canoe load of Pottawatomies crossing the mouth of Green Bay was overtaken by a gale, shipwrecked and the whole crew drowned."[57] At this point we cannot say whether this is ridiculously brief, or closer to fact than many longer versions.

Each of the two 1881 recitals of the legend is dignified by inclusion in a serious history. We give the versions in full, inviting the reader to join the game and share the fun of detecting their common features, both obvious and subtle. A weighty *History of Northern Wisconsin*[58] in its chapter on Door County gives the following as "Traditional and Early History":

"Porte des Morts - 'The Door of Death' - has been closed to the navigator of northern Lake Michigan by the construction of the canal, but tradition still keeps alive a story of many who passed through never to return. When the Jesuit fathers were battling for the cross 200 years ago in Brown County, it is said that the Pottawatomies made Washington Island their rendezvous, obtaining their game from the peninsula just across the way. All Indian tribes are more jealous of their hunting grounds than they are of their wives, and the Pottawatomies were no exception to the rule. When they heard, therefore, that the Chippewas had invaded their territory, and were ruthlessly cutting off their base of supplies, they assembled their braves in a mighty flotilla of canoes, which drew up in battle array upon the west shore of Detroit Island, just south of Washington. While midway in their passage across 'Death's Door,' but by that name then unknown, a furious white squall came galloping over the waters from the south, rushed upon their frail barks and scattered them to the winds, and the warriors to their graves. For many days the bodies were washed upon the shores of Detroit Island, and the waiters and watchers there buried their dead and deserted the fearful region of desolation. Fate, or, in other words, the Evil Spirit, had favored the fortunes of the Chippewas. It had rushed from the bluffs of the land they occupied and destroyed the flower of the Pottawatomies. The place from whence it came is called Evil Spirit Point, and seldom it is that an Indian of the Pottawatomie tribe will be found within a day's journey of the Door of Death."

Newspaperman Charles I. Martin's little *History of DOOR COUNTY, Wisconsin*[59] took book form in spring of 1881, but had previously reached the public's hands through weekly installments in Martin's *EXPOSITOR*. The editor tells us..."The town of Washington was the first organized town in the county, and in going there to gather facts for this history, we had occasion to cross that passage of water so widely known as 'Death's Door,' and right here is probably a suitable place to comment on the origin of

DEATH'S DOOR

"The name 'Death's Door' or *Port du mort* has its origin in an Indian tradition, which is probably founded in fact. Some two hundred years ago Washington Island was the headquarters of the Pottawottamie Indians. Here was their home, and about the harbors and bays of the islands, their fishing grounds. Just across, upon the main land, was their principal hunting ground. Crossing from the island in their canoes, they secured plenty of deer for meat and moccasins; an intrusion upon these hunting grounds by any other Indian tribe was at once resisted, and many bloody battles were fought near the lower end of the peninsula. On the occasion to which the tradition refers, the Chippewas had been for some time killing game upon the peninsula, and every effort to drive them away had proved futile. Finally the Pottawattamies determined to make a final and bloody effort to drive the invaders off. They mustered every brave in the tribe able to draw a bow or throw a tomahawk; every canoe belonging to the tribe was brought into service to take them over. The flotilla of birch bark started on its expedition of death, one August afternoon, embarking at the westerly side of Detroit Island, and attempting to cross to the main land, preparatory to making an attack under the cover of the night upon the camp of the Chippewas. When about one half way across the 'Door,' a 'white squall,' such as is common in those regions, rushed down from the bluffs of the main land, struck the fleet and upset the canoes, drowning every able-bodied man of the Pottawattamie tribes. That passage of water was called in the Indian language the *Door of Death*. The missionaries rendered it in French 'Port du mort' which, in English, gives us 'Death's Door.' The dead bodies of the drowned braves were driven ashore upon Detroit Island at the place of embarkation. A place was cleared at this point, and all were buried there; but the burial was very shallow probably owing to there being no able-bodied men left in the tribe to do the work. Several persons now living in Door County have visited this burying ground, and report that no longer than fifteen or twenty years ago many human bones could be seen sticking out of the grass and lying upon the surface of the ground. The Indians supposed the squall to be the breath of an evil spirit which resided in the bluff from whence the squall came; hence they called it Skillagalee (Evil Spirit) point. The remnant of the Pottawattamies soon left the Island. The story soon became known among all the tribes in this region, and all believed that the 'Evil Spirit' was disposed to take vengeance upon all Indians coming upon the Islands. For this reason Indians are never or hardly ever found upon any of the Islands of the Door."

The similarities need no pointing out; clearly one version was taken from the other. And with Martin's published some months before the bigger volume, we must

25

assume it borrowed from him.[60] At any rate, we find in 1881 some details which strongly suggest that Fox in 1915 drew upon these texts.

We have searched backward nearly ninety years, penetrating a short way into this region's pioneer period. The findings may be distilled into this: All of the full-length versions at hand of the Death's Door legend seem to be essentially white men's stories about Indians, showing strong evidence of dramatization, and remarkable variations concerning some basic elements (direction of the great wind, names of tribes involved, warfare or none). They are hardly acceptable as faithful re-tellings of an aboriginal history or tale. But neither, on the other hand, do they seem to be wholly fabrications or fictions; somewhere out of sight behind them, we find ourselves feeling, there must lie at least a word of truth. We take up the search for that word.

As with any aging trail, this one offers a fading footprint and a weakening scent. We examine every promising sign; and sometimes even the false clues are interesting. We find one in 1875, when Mr. Littlejohn in his *Legends*[61] recites a tale which he sets in 1803:

The Foxes, Sauk and Chippewas from around Green Bay brought war against the Ottawas in Michigan, but their campaign failed, costing them heavy losses. The Chippewas then turned against their allies, and massed ten thousand warriors on Lake Superior, and "a further levy of five thousand were in camp on the north shore of Lake Michigan west of the Mackinaw Straits, destined to enter Green Bay with a fleet of canoes." But under the young Sauk chief Red Wing, the allies slaughtered one army of five thousand Chippewas near Escanaba. Meanwhile, five thousand of the Lake Superior Chippewas entered Green Bay by the Menominee River, and the five thousand others by way of the Sault and Mackinaw, "and crossing, landed on its west shore a few miles north of the entrance of the Menominee."

This story, laid well within the historical period but unsupported by any accepted history and highly improbable in the numbers of warriors involved, is clearly gleaned "along the uncertain, misty line" of which Littlejohn spoke. But it is another of the white men's stories about Indians in this region, which shares at least some elements of the Death's Door legend.

With the Civil War three years past, an official of the government's Indian Department, Thomas L. McKenney, refers to a Lake Michigan storm which killed six hundred canoe-borne Winnebagoes.[62] Before we consider in full this lugubrious record, may we lay it aside for a brief one hundred forty-seven years?

In 1854 appears a variant of the legend which is arresting both for a wholly new twist, and for the personality and position of its teller. James Jesse Strang, at that time both a representative in the Michigan legislature and King of the Mormon colony on Beaver Island, says:

"Pontiac, failing in his attack on Detroit, went to the west of Lake Michigan and rallied an immense army, who encountered a severe storm on Lake Michigan, and their canoes were broken in pieces against the rocks south of Death's Door, and nearly all his warriors perished. Their destruction is written in hieroglyphics on the rocks."[63]

As the reprint's editor points out: "...Strang is confused...An old tradition, which Strang may have somehow associated with Pontiac, says that a party of Potawatomi Indians was annihilated by a band of Winnebagoes in Death Door..."

While Strang most probably found mention of "hieroglyphics on the rocks" in a book of 1851,[64] there exists a possibility that he actually saw them himself. In the turmoil following his election to the legislature in 1851,

27

Strang, by the surprising move of traveling from Beaver Island to Lansing by way of Green Bay, foiled an attempt to prevent his reaching the state capital. He may have passed through Death's Door.[65]

In July of 1847 the editor of the Albany *Evening Journal*, one Thurlow Weed, on a steamship pleasure cruise "for $2 per day, including board", points out " 'Death's Door,' a narrow strait, with several reefs (where it is said a large tribe of Indians, endeavoring to escape from a hostile tribe in canoes, were all drowned)... forms the entrance to a group of wild, picturesque islands..."[66] Weed was in a company of Easterners who must have been strangers to this region; almost certainly no Green Bay Indians were among them. Possibly the captain or mate was familiar with the legend and passed it along.

August, 1839 finds Douglass Houghton, State Geologist of Michigan, traveling through these waters making a geological survey. He notes in his diary:

"Passage des Mort or Death's Door is reputed to take its name from a war party of indians, in canoes, having been driven against the bold and lofty cliffs, in a severe storm -. All excepting 3 or 4 are said to have perished-"[67]

Occasionally it is the word of a common man, a comparative unknown, which sheds the most light. Early in 1835, twenty-six-year-old New York farmer Nelson Olin sought fortune in the young western city of Milwaukee. That October he was a fellow passenger with Solomon Juneau ("at $2.50 per head" round trip) on a sailing vessel to the government land sale at Green Bay. On the return...

"When coming out of the bay into the lake near Death's Door, we encountered a terrible storm, with high winds and a very rough sea. The bow of the boat ran onto a rock, high and dry. [Quick work with the capstan, a rope and two broomsticks pried them back into deep water and on their way.] If we had not had the broomsticks on board, we would in all probability have been shipwrecked and dashed against the rocks and shared the same fate as the Indians did who gave it the name of Death's Door. Juneau said there were a hundred Indians dashed against those rocks and killed in a single storm."[68]

To this point, this is the nearest approach to a documented statement from an Indian source concerning historic facts behind the legend. The context shows "Juneau" to be Milwaukee's pioneer, Solomon Juneau. The latter, not an Indian himself, had close personal ties with them all his adult life; also, the water journey between Milwaukee and Green Bay was not new to him.[69] His opportunities for familiarity with the Death's Door locality and its aboriginal history were outstanding. If we assume that Olin reports him with accuracy, we may take particular note of three details: "a hundred Indians" - far fewer battered victims than satisfy some other writers; "the Indians...gave it the name of Death's Door" - a forceful verification of Indian origin; and - no mention is made by Juneau (according to Olin) of war, battle, flight or pursuit. Of course, we must face the possibility that Olin's account is an abridgement, if not a distortion, of Juneau's remarks; but in the century and a third now covered, no mention commends itself to our credence so strongly as this.

At the 1834 marker we reach the legend's version attributed in Holand's 1917 footnote to surveyor John Brink:

"The Indians say that a whole tribe of Indians, 300 in number, lost their lives one night near the big bluff that is called 'Death's Door,' and that is why the spot was given such a dismal name. As the story goes the tribe was to land in canoes near the spot where they are said to have lost their lives and surprise their enemies, who were encamped near by. They were betrayed, however, by one of their number who was to notify them by a fire on the beach as to the best

place to make the landing. Instead of building the fire on a hill about a quarter of a mile further up the lake, the signal was placed on the bluff, and when the 300 Injuns attempted to make the landing at 'Death's Door' they were dashed against rocks and perished. That is how the spot is said to have obtained its name."

There is no question that Brink surveyed Township lines in Door County in spring of 1834.[70] The present writer confesses frustration at his lack of success in locating Brink's legend anywhere but in Holand's footnote, and at the historian's failure to confide its whereabouts. But he has no choice but to accept it as given. In that form, it seems to be the seed from which Holand's dramatization flowered; the "spy" and "signal fire" elements appear nowhere else.

Weighing the Brink version against its closest contemporaries (and against the earlier mentions still to be examined) we can only believe that Brink fancied himself as a tale-spinner as did several later writers, or that he heard the story from such an entertainer, Indian or white.

In summer of 1831, Samuel Stambaugh, United States Indian agent at Green Bay, on instructions from the War Department, reported on the northeastern Wisconsin area. From the tone of his detailed descriptions it seems likely that he toured it himself. He says of our vicinity:

"The nearest channel to the main land...is known to mariners by the name of *Death's Door* passage. It received this name, as an Indian tradition informs us, in consequence of a circumstance occurring many years ago, by which a large body of Indians were lost near the bluff of rocks projecting over the Lake at this point... A band of Indians in canoes, on their way to some of the French Trading posts, halted at this place for the purpose of resting and taking some refreshment, and while seated on their stone table, which then projected about three feet above the surface of the water, a storm arose suddenly, which swept over the rock a tremendous sea, and dashed their canoes to pieces. The bluff of rocks was too steep to scale, and the poor creatures, having no other means of escape, but trusting to the waves to drive them ashore at some distance from the fatal spot, nearly all perished. On the face of the rocks fifteen or twenty feet above the surface of the water,

31

there are figures of Indians and Canoes painted Indian fashion, which must have been done with much difficulty, and by the help of scaling ladders, during a dead calm on the Lake."[71]

Apart from Stambaugh's official position and his contact with many Indians, the noteworthy point here is the complete absence of any hint of tribal war.

The illustrious Henry Rowe Schoolcraft, traveling down from Green Bay by canoe in 1825, noted in his journal on September first that he camped "at the Little Detroit, or strait, so called, in the Grand Traverse" and observed "There are some hieroglyphics on the rocks." Farmer's 1830 map shows Schoolcraft's route through the area; his failure to refer to the Death's Door name or legend may be disturbing, but his mention of the "hieroglyphics" (the earliest word we find of them) whets our interest. The brief's error apparently traces to Farmer's 1830 map, which, according to *WisBrief,* 165, showed "Schoolcraft's Route in 1820." From Schoolcraft's own account in *Travels* (Albany, 1821), and from other trustworthy sources, it is clear that in 1820 he toured Green Bay by canoe only from the Fox River's mouth to the Sturgeon Bay portage, and was in Chicago on September first, never having approached Death's Door. But Schoolcraft's *Personal Memoirs* shows that in August, 1825, he attended the "grand council or treaty" with the tribes, held by Michigan's Gov. Cass and Missouri's Gen. Clark at Prairie du Chien, then made his way back east by canoe, reaching Death's Door and the islands on September first.[72]

Mid-September in 1817 found Samuel Storrow, Judge Advocate in the United States Army, passing our islands in an open boat, accompanied by a guide and interpreter, and by Lt. John Pierce, who a year before had sailed through these waters and tarried on Washington Island.[73] Since the interpreter knew by sight and name an

Indian chief living on Detroit Island, these men must have served as expert advisors, yet Storrow touches only lightly on the legend, and mentions war not at all:

"...we reached . . . the southerly cape of Green Bay, Port des Morts, so called from the destruction at this place of a number of the Pottowotomies. The cape itself is high and perpendicular. We encamped under the precipice on a small margin, the water washing the foot of our tent."[74]

The *Wisconsin Magazine of History* preserves for us the entertaining observations of Willard Keyes of Vermont as he travels toward Green Bay by canoe a month before Storrow.[75] In August the Yankee passes our "numerous islands, with remarkable precipices," camps "on an island they call 'Petite Detroit' (little Streight)" where lives a band of Indians "employed in building Birch Bark Canoes, and weaving flag mats." He observes "point 'De Mort' (or point of Death) so called from the many Indian canoes wrecked there in attempting to pass the point which is perpendicular -rocks rising out of the water." Again we find in the legend no mention of inter-tribal strife.

Another two-thirds of a century searched has uncovered legend versions notably briefer and less florid than those nearer our own day. Except for obvious aberrations (like Strang's introduction of Pontiac into the story) they tend toward increasing agreement on a few basic elements. And several mentions during this period have been conspicuous for the character, position and high professional repute of their reporters.

Now we search the record of almost one hundred years more for a word which bears on our legend; then we find, not a word, but a pageant:

In the 1720's the Fox Indians in what is to become Wisconsin are a source of "trouble and disorder" to the French, and Louis XV, "persuaded of the necessity of

33

destroying that nation" grants "sixty millions of livres... for the expenses of that war, news of the success of which he will be expecting with impatience."[76] It is intriguing to contemplate this scratch of a quill in Versailles launching a force which would eventually wash against a bluff at the Porte des Morts.

A company of some four hundred French troops was joined by "eight or nine hundred savages," and all set out from Montreal under the command of the Sieur de Lignery. As chaplain to the French went a Flemish Recollect missionary, the Reverend Father Emanuel Crespel, to whom we are grateful for the record.[77] On the fourteenth of August in 1728 this colorful force, having come in canoes eleven hundred miles from Montreal, was passing our islands and, says Crespel:

"...as we were doubling Cap a la Mort, which is about five leagues across, we encountered a gust of wind, which drove ashore several canoes that were unable to double a point in order to obtain a shelter; they were broken by the shock; and we were obliged to distribute among the other canoes the men who, by the greatest good fortune in the world, had all escaped from the danger."

Here, in "Cap a la Mort," is the earliest suggestion of the Death's Door name which this writer has found. We notice that the chaplain, though in company with hundreds of Indians, gives no intimation of the legend save the disturbing name (possibly because his companions lived far east of this region and were ignorant of its folklore). Since Crespel appears to speak of an established geographical entity, and death does not touch this expedition, there is no hint that the passage was named on this day. This mishap, then (in which the near-victims were probably white men) seems unlikely as the original source of the legend. But we believe this occurrence - and other occasions of catastrophe in the Death's Door area - influenced the telling and re-telling of the legend by many men over many years.

In July of 1721 a well-known Jesuit historian, Pierre Francois Xavier de Charlevoix, commissioned by the French government to seek a route to the Western Sea, passed through Green Bay's waters, noting the islands' characteristics as he went. He does not mention the legend or Death's Door, nor name the latter on his map. But at the fort near the Bay's head he meets the Winnebagoes (called Puans or Otchagras) who he says suffered the following at some time in the past:

"...they undertook to revenge the defeat which they had suffered from the Illinois; but that Enterprise caused them a new loss, from which they have not recovered. Six hundred of their best Men had embarked to seek their Enemy; but while they were crossing Lake Michigan they were surprised by a furious gale, which caused them all to perish."[78]

Although this debacle appears to occur somewhere south of the Death's Door region, it does seem accepted as fact by well-known historians of the 1700's as well as of our century. In the light of the evident flexibility of the legend under varying influences, it seems likely that this happening had, at the very least, some effect on later recitals of the Death's Door legend, by white men and possibly by Indians; surely it contains elements which *could* have been used in constructing the legend we know.

In searching backward for an ancient source for the legend, we find not only a distressing paucity of clues as we approach the earliest historic period, but another disquieting fact: there is an imposing number of recorded and probable visitors to this region who might be expected to refer to the name but do not.

Thus in 1774 Peter Pond and his party, though passing our islands in a "small fleat" of canoes, mentions nothing more sinister than "the Mouth of the Bay which is two or three Mile Brod."[79] And thus Jonathan Carver, who from his canoe examines this "ftring of iflands" and spends a September night in 1766 as guest in "a town of the Ottawaws" on "the largeft and beft" (which can hardly be other than Washington Island) says only this of the passages between Lake and Bay:

"The communications between lake Michigan and the Green Bay, has been reported by fome to be impracticable for the paffage of veffels larger than canoes or boats, on account of the fhoals that lie between the iflands of the Grand Traverfe; but on founding it, I found fufficient depth for a veffel of fixty tons, and the breadth proportionable."[80]

It cannot escape us that Carver's careful scrutiny of waterways which included Death's Door[81] says nothing (and his map shows nothing) of the forbidding name. Another Carver comment is thought-provoking:

"The French, whilft they retained their power in North America, had taken every artful method to keep other nations, particularly the English, in ignorance of the concerns of the interior parts of it; and to accomplish this defign with the greater certainty, they had publifhed innacurate maps and falfe accounts (etc.) whether - to prevent thefe nations from being difcovered and traded with, or to conceal their difcourse, - I will not determine; but whatfoever was the cause from which it arofe, it tended to miflead."[82]

It is customary to say, as does Holand: "The French early adopted the Indian name of the channel and translated it into Porte des Morts - Death's Door."[83] It seems logical, then, to look for the Indian name as a clue to the legend itself. Unfortunately, but one lonely reference has been revealed to this searcher, that one from testimony of two Indian witnesses, mother and son, in the 1925 boundary dispute.

Mary Ann and Dave Cota claimed lifelong familiarity with this locality, including "the Door, the Indian for which was Kee bi skjonan."[84] Verification and explanation of this appellation was pursued through Wisconsin's largest libraries, where numerous books of place-names and Indian names yielded nothing. Experts from Sault Sainte Marie, Michigan, and Chicago's Newberry Library could find no "Death's Door" meaning in the phrase. Door County's own Chief Roy Oshkosh wrote us: "The word... I do not know...and I cannot find it in any book..."[85]

Our lack of success in seeking a verifiable Indian name for Death's Door, plus the early appearance of a French version, impels us to consider Carver's suspicions seriously. Dare we suggest that French fur traders, hoping to discourage English competition, might have attached a forbidding name to the entrance to Green Bay? But if so, how does one explain later mentions by honest reporters of "ancient Indian tradition" and similar references? Let us see.

For reasons carefully outlined in Blair's *Indian Tribes* it is evident that by the nineteenth century the tribesmen were known to "cite, as belonging to their primitive beliefs, certain facts of which neither Perrot or the Jesuit missionaries found, even one hundred years ago, the slightest trace in the traditions of these peoples."[86] The Indians, in other words, might have recited a legend which their ancestors had absorbed much earlier from the Europeans just as they had adopted the use of glass beads, metal hatchets, and alcoholic drinks.

In early autumn of 1698 a priest of the Seminary of Quebec, Jean Francois Buisson de St. Cosme, left "L'Isle du

Detour" west of Mackinac and in canoes "crossed from island to island" at the entrance to Green Bay. Despite his expressed interest in the Bay's waters and in the Indian tribes around them, he says nothing of an Indian legend or name for the dangerous strait.[87]

This omission gains importance when we consider that in St. Cosme's party was the famous Henri de Tonty, La Salle's lieutenant whose personal knowledge of the Grand Traverse and Door peninsula region had begun some eighteen years before, following the *Griffin's* historic voyage into these waters. The present writer finds neither Death's Door mention nor reference to a legend in the literature dealing with Tonty's travels and narratives.[88] Nor is there mention by Hennepin or the others who in "four Canoùs" accompanied La Salle southward from "the Ifland of the Poutouatamis" across Death's Door to the mainland in 1679.[89] Had the fearsome name been current in Indian dialect or in French at the time, it would seem in character for Hennepin to have seized the opportunity to use such a dramatic reference.

During roughly the final third of the seventeenth century, forest-rover Nicholas Perrot was often in close contact with the Indians of the Green Bay region; yet his *Memoire* does not mention the legend nor a name for the treacherous passage.[90] The travels and labors hereabouts of the Jesuit missionaries Allouez and Andre and the more fleeting passage of Father Marquette, all carefully noted in the Jesuit *Relations*, give no hint of the legend.[91]

The visit of Radisson and Grosseilliers to quite possibly this precise locality in the late 1650's is recorded without identification of the strait or mention of a legend.[92] And in the 1634-1635 accounts of the man whose very name marks the beginning of history in Lake Michigan and Green Bay - Jean Nicolet - the record is bare.

We are groping near the "uncertain, misty line" told of in the beginning; written history can lead us backward no farther. The 1600's and early 1700's tell us nothing definite of Death's Door name or legend. (It need hardly be said that absence of mention is by itself no proof of nonexistence; conceivably one might view the Taj Mahal and not write of it in a diary. But can we reasonably ignore the apparently complete absence of any indication in the first ninety-four years of the historic period?) The writer of history must endure with a mingling of hope and trepidation the abiding possibility that evidence, either freshly-unearthed or merely overlooked by him, may at any time force a dramatic revision of his findings. But at this moment of writing we must conclude the following:

Our name of Death's Door for the southernmost natural passage from Lake Michigan into Green Bay clearly follows the French *Porte des Morts*, which was attached to the waterway possibly in the 1600's but more probably around 1700.

While *Porte* may perhaps have followed a poetic Indian name, it as possibly was coined by the French on their canoe-borne travels.

The legend as we know it today is a mixture of motifs - modern, frontier American, early French, and probably even aboriginal.

Beyond question the Death's Door legend refuses to die. Indeed, within recent times it has done better than stay alive. Nurtured by modern minstrels who bathe it in vivid color, it has gained the vigor to change and to grow. Hear how in the 1940's it drew from twisted ancient roots the strength to thrust itself toward tomorrow:

"Indian canoeists dreaded this passage, and the French, who came after Nicolet's voyage in 1634...learned to share their fear. It is supposed that Robert La Salle's *Griffon*, first sailing vessel on the Great Lakes, was.

wrecked here in 1679, while carrying furs from Washington Island to a post just above Niagara Falls. Some sailors on the Great Lakes still insist that the vessel did not go down. The *Griffon* or its ghost, they say, has been seen scudding over the water in the teeth of a never-ending gale that blew up at Death's Door more than 250 years ago.[93]

In Hjalmar Holand's several "Legend of Death's Door" accounts (in his 1917 *History of Door County*; in several editions of *Old Peninsula Days*, 1925 to 1959; in *Peninsula Historical Review* of December, 1928; and in a Sturgeon Bay newspaper of May 26, 1916) details vary so materially as to preclude any possible claim to historical accuracy. From his pen the "Legend" emerges as a collection of literary exercises reflecting the author's casual recollections at any given moment. Examination of the many versions bequeathed us by other bards serves largely to reinforce the image of the Legend as a fiction by English-speaking white men, often composed with a keen eye for dramatic effect but with cavalier disdain for the chores of historical research.

We find the Legend's tragedy placed "shortly after...1634" in Holand's *Old Peninsula Days* eighth edition of 1959, but around 1766 in his article of May 26, 1916. Another writer's newspaper piece in 1934 (see note 37) puts it near the time of George Washington's birth in 1732; and "A.R." in the *Door County Advocate* of December 4, 1879 has it "About the time of the first settlement..." - which *may* mean the mid-1830's. Among the many Legend versions a similar lack of agreement appears in naming the tribes involved, and Holand's own stories show little consistency among themselves.

Similar looseness is evident in many statements concerning the source of the Death's Door name. Thus Holand tells us that "early French explorers...discovered that the door or passage...from Lake Michigan to Green Bay at the extremity of the Door County Peninsula was an extremely dangerous passage. They therefore called it Porte des Morts - the Door of Death."[94] In the same work he says: "The French early adopted the Indian name of the channel and translated it into Porte des Morts - Death's Door."[95]

Another example of assumption indulged in for dramatic effect appeared in *Literary Digest* of September 9,

1922: "Porte des Mortes - the Door of Death - so named by early French navigators who saw many a boat go down in the storms which drove sailing vessels into the danger-fraught passage." The apparent confusions in this chilling scenario merit analysis: Unless "early French navigators" means voyageurs, French sailors were virtually unknown in these waters after the *Griffin's* unique voyage in 1679; and the voyageurs managed large canoes not classified as sailing vessels and rarely involved in documented losses near Death's Door. Following the brief 1816 appearance of American sailing vessels in this region (on which two Green Bay residents of French blood served as pilots) the sailing craft which eventually suffered "many" losses near the Door from the mid-1800's to early 1900's were essentially a part of American - certainly not "early French" - navigation.

Despite the obvious defects in the Legend as it comes down to us, there remains the possibility or even the likelihood that some probably minor occurrence in Indian history was the seed from which the white man's Legend grew and flourished!

FOOTNOTES:

1. F.J. Littlejohn, Northwestern Bible and Publishing Co. (Allegan, Michigan, 1875; reprint, Allegan County Historical Society, 1956).
2. The Merriam-Webster New International Dictionary (Springfield, Mass., 1951).
3. From foreword by Charles E. Brown to *Wisconsin Indian Place Legends*, Folklore Section, Federal Writers' Projects (Madison, 1936).
4. William D. Lyman, "Indian Myths of the Northwest," p. 377 in *Proceedings of the American Antiquarian Society*, New Series, Vol. 25 (Worcester, Mass., 1915).
5. *Discovery and Exploration of the Mississippi Valley* (New York, 1853).
6. Rhode Island v. Massachusetts; p, 269 of *WisBrief.*
7. *The Fate of the Griffon* (Chicago, 1974). No matter which of the islands at the mouth of Green Bay gave anchorage to La Salle's vessel, it had to lie north of the Death's Door strait. And when the *Griffin* "... failed the 18th of September with a wefterly Wind, and fir'd a Gun to take their leave," she was headed in a generally northeasterly direction toward Mackinac and away from Death's Door. In 1974 Harrison John MacLean believed that he had established the site of the ship's remains in a secluded cove near Tobermory, Ontario.
8. Hennepin, *A New Discovery* (Thwaites edition, Chicago, 1903), I:122.
9. *Sailing Directions for Lake Michigan, Green Bay and the Strait of Mackinac* (GPO, Washington, 1906).
10. Bulletin No. 33, U. S. Lake Survey Office, 1924; quoted in *WisBrief,* 171, The final change from sail to steam had failed to earn a good name for the waterway .
11. One chart of disasters in Door County waters gives name and type of vessel, cargo, year, fate and location; many of the wrecks lie in the Porte des Morts passage. ("Frederickson's Chart," etc., Frankfort, Michigan, 1959; printed by *Door County Advocate.*)
12. Michigan Exhibit 166: "Extracts from an article written by Dr. John J. Sherman, of Marinette, Wisconsin, February 1902."
13. A. C. and L. F. Frederickson. *Ships and Shipwrecks in Door County, Wisconsin, Volume Two* (Frankfort, 1963), 70. Mention of light of "Plum" is an apparent slip; it was not then in operation.
14. A. C. Wheeler, *The Chronicles of Milwaukee* (Milwaukee, 1861), 63.
15. This should read "Pilot Island"; during these years Plum Island had no operating lighthouse. *A Gleam Across the Wave*, Arthur and

Evelyn Knudsen (Sturgeon Bay, c. 1949), 49, 63; also *MichBrief* and *WisBrief.*

16. Beers, *History of the Great Lakes ,I* (Chicago, 1899)"A memorable storm…"; see also *Gleam*, 36.

17. Personal interview, June, 1967.

18. *WisBrief*, 163-64. In 1967 Plum Island's two range lights are colored red.

19. The figures concerning appropriation for and cost of the Death's Door light are from an 1871 government compilation of lighthouse and related information, cited in *WisBrief*, 183. Michigan's Exhibit 109 is treated in *MichBrief*, 166. Also, we mistakenly assumed that "Tail Point Entrance to Green Bay" referred to the Death's Door region; it probably concerned a slim peninsula a few miles north of Green Bay city.

20. In the 1925 boundary dispute Michigan offered photos of old ruins and testimony by men familiar with Washington Island. The Wolverine lawyers confessed, however: "There is no record at all of the old light on Plum Island." Our facts concerning lighthouses come largely from the two briefs (which do not always agree). Witnesses in the trial record include: "Captain Peterson (C. O. Pedersen), Fred Richter, Captain Betts, William McDonald, Jacob Young, Martin Knudson, James K. Allger, Captain Frank D. Root." Concerning the chronology of lighthouses in Death's Door (see page 7 and footnotes 19-21) the evidence is in some respects conflicting and confusing. Most tantalizing is the suggestion of an early light on Plum Island, pre-dating the 1850 Pilot Island beacon. Both briefs in the boundary dispute conclude that an "old" light must have stood for a time on Plum, though no official record at hand proves it. Some other sources bearing on the matter: *Door County Advocate*, June 25, 1885; H. R. Holand, "The Forgotten Lighthouse" in *Peninsula Historical Review* (December, 1928), 68; Holand, *Old Peninsula Days* (8th edition, 1959), 88; Knudsen, *Gleam* (see note 15), 49-50; Alexander Winchell (Wisconsin Exhibit 368 in boundary dispute). Our best guess is that the old stone lighthouse operated on Plum Island, possibly from about 1848 to 1858.

21. For more tales of thrilling shipwrecks and rescues, plus a pleasant taste of nineteenth century life and work on this water-washed rock in the eastern end of the passage, see *A Gleam Across the Wave* (note 15). See also the *Advocate* article by Ben Fagg, reprinted in Hjalmar R. Holand, *History of Door County, Wisconsin,I* (Chicago, 1917), 257-8.

22. Herbert J. Sanderson, *Pictorial Marine History* (Sturgeon Bay, 1942).

23. Jesse Miner, unpublished manuscript, "Mail carrying, etc." See Eaton, *Washington Island 1836-1876.*

24. See note 23.

25. *Door County Advocate,* Mar. 2, 1876.

26. *Door County Advocate,* Feb. 20, 1879.

27. *Door County Advocate,* Mar.18, 1880.

28. *Door County Advocate,* Jan. 31, 1884.

29. *Door County Advocate,* Feb., 1885

30. William Snow Miller, M.D., "Dr. Thordur Gudmundsen/The Icelandic Doctor of Washington Island," in *Wisconsin Medical Journal,* May, 1939, 404-408.

31. September 4, 1958. The paddler, Dudley Canfield, built the kayak of Sitka spruce frames, canvas-covered and airplane-doped. Eleven feet overall, three in the beam, it weighed forty pounds, was propelled the five and one-half miles in an hour and a half through slightly choppy water.

32. *Door County Advocate,* March 15, 1935

33. The phrase in the Michigan Enabling Act of 1836.

34. Holand, *Door County,I*, 38-39 and George R. Fox, "Indian Remains on Washington Island" in *Wisconsin Archeologist,* 13:169-171 (January, 1915).

35. William Barry Furlong, "Door County, Wisconsin," in *Venture,* October/November, 1966.

36. Robert E. Gard and L. G. Sorden (New York, 1962), 177-178.

37. Dolores and Ed Allen, *The Key to the Door Peninsula* (Sturgeon Bay), 53.

38. Robert Morris, article on Door County.

39. No date, copyright, place or publisher.

40. Fred L. Holmes, ed., *Wisconsin* (Chicago, 1946), II:357.

41. (Eau Claire, 1944), 221-2.

42. (Indianapolis-New York, 1944), 321, 328.

43. In *Jacobsen's Book of Poems* (Washington Island). It is pleasant to learn that a reprint has appeared in 1967, bound together with equally welcome reprints of Miner's *Early Days on Washington Island* and the Knudsens' *Gleam.*

44. Folklore Section, Federal Writers' Projects (Madison, 1936), 8-9.

45. Presumably by James Weber Linn; the present writer has seen only typed copies and cannot document its publication precisely.

46. In Local History Room, Milwaukee Pubic Library.

47. (Garden City, N. Y., 1929), 116.
48. Vol. 19, No. 2, 41ff.
49. J. P. Schumacher, "Indian Remains in Door County," in Vol. 16, No. 4, 144-145.
50. Sydney W. Jackman and John F. Freeman, eds., *The Journal of David Bates Douglass*; Marquette, Northern Michigan University Press, 1969, 110.
51. Henry Rowe Schoolcraft, *The Indian in His Wigwam*, Buffalo, 1848, 93-94.
52. *Milwaukee Sentinel*, Oct. 6, 1958, "Jacobsen Museum Traces Washington Island Saga."
53. See note 34.
54. See note 34.
55. *Lake Michigan*, 328.
56. Fox, "Indian Remains." His uncertainty regarding the tribes is reflected on page 159: "Little is known as to what Red tribes originally occupied Washington Island. The western shore of Lake Michigan up through the Door peninsula and these islands was Pottawatomie country...The narrations of the Jesuits locate the Noquet in this region when the French first came."
57. Deborah B. Martin, *History of Brown County, Wisconsin* (Chicago, 1913), 9.
58. The Western Historical Co., (Chicago, 1881), 225.
59. *Together with Biographies of Nearly Seven Hundred Families, and Mention of 4,000 Persons* (Sturgeon Bay, 1881), 19-21.
60. In their Preface, dated December, 1881, the Chicago editors wistfully explained they were struggling to get the printing done "before the severe Winter weather set in."
61. 435ff.; see note 1.
62. With James Hall, *History of the Indian Tribes of North America*, etc., (Philadelphia, 1868), III : 116.
63. *Ancient and Modern Michilimackinac*, etc., (Beaver Island, 1854), 13-14. In 1959 W. Stewart Woodfill of Mackinac Island published a splendid reprint edited by George S. May of the Michigan Historical Commission.
64. The 1851 book Strang could have seen is Schooolcraft's *Personal Memoirs*.
65. On another occasion Strang may have had dealings on Washington Island, may even have set foot upon it. (Letter of J. E. Wells in *Northern Islander*, December 6, 1855.)
66. Beers, *Great Lakes, I*, 212.

67. Wisconsin Exhibit 54; Archives-Manuscripts Room, Library of State Historical Society of Wisconsin.

68. "Reminiscences of Milwaukee in 1835-36," in *Wisconsin Magazine of History*, 13: 215-216. Juneau's granddaughter, Isabella Fox, writes: "1835 -August, the first title to land upon which now stands the city of Milwaukee, was obtained by Solomon Juneau at the land sale held at Green Bay." (*Solomon Juneau: A Biography*; Milwaukee, 1916), 216. The Green Bay land sale took place between July 30 and August 9, 1835.

69. *WHC* XI: 244; *Wisconsin Magazine of History*, 50:37 (Autumn, 1966).

70. Township surveys in Register of Deeds Office, Door County Court House.

71. *WHC* . XV, 423-424.

72. Fox, "Indian Remains" (see note 34), speaks of "Pictograph rocks . . . on the rocky bluff near Death's Door." Whether or not Indians drew on a bluff some illustrations or record of the legend remains in the area of conjecture. The September first quotation is from Schoolcraft's *Personal Memoirs of a Residence of Thirty Years with the Indian Tribes*, etc., (Philadelphia, 1851), 226. Both briefs in the boundary dispute set this visit in 1820, which seems to be in error. Confusion is easy, for in summer, 1820 Schoolcraft saw Green Bay with the Cass expedition; he spent summer, 1825 with the Cass-Clark expedition, and again reached Green Bay. (C. S. and S. Osborn, *Schoolcraft-Longfellow-Hiawatha*; Lancaster, Pa., 1942; 563-565.)

73. Pierce's younger brother Franklin became the fourteenth President of the United States; for more on the lieutenant see *The NAMING*, 8, 16, 22.

74. *WHC* VI : 166.

75. "A Journal of Life in Wisconsin One Hundred Years Ago," in *Wisconsin Magazine of History*, 3:348.

76. From letter of the King to Canada's Governor-General, quoted in *WHC* V: 86.

77. In *WHC* V: 87-88. DeLignery's official report said, "... Our army was composed of nearly twelve hundred savages and four hundred and fifty French..." (*WHC* XVII: 32). *WHC* X: 47-53 gives another translation of Crespel's account.

78. *Journal Historique* (Paris, 1744); quoted in *WHC* XVI: 412 and in III: 286. French historian Bacqueville de la Potherie's *Histoire* (Paris, 1722) tells the same story with variations; quoted in *WHC* XVI: 4. Louise Phelps Kellogg's *The French Regime in Wisconsin and the*

Northwest (Madison, 1925) seems to accept the latter; p. 88. The editors of *WHC* XVI place these events between 1640 and 1660.

79. *WHC* XVIII: 329.

80. Jonathan Carver, *Three Years Travels through the Interior Parts of North America,* etc., (Edinburgh, 1798), 34.

81. The map titled *A Plan of Captain Carver's Travels,* etc., shows his route by a dotted line, which seems to skirt Washington Island's east side, scurries into the east channel, runs through Detroit Harbor, and escapes toward Death's Door and Green Bay. Elsewhere he describes "the pipe of peace, which was fixed at the head of my canoe, and the English colours that were flying at the stern."

82. Quote from Carver, *Travels,* 21. This matter is interestingly dealt with in *WHC* IV: 227-229.

83. Holand, *Door County,* 40n. The earliest English versions of the Death's Door name we have found are from Keyes in 1817 (*point of Death*) and Stambaugh in 1831 (*Death's door passage*). Also in 1817 appear both Keyes' *point De Mort* and Storrow's *Port des Morts,* which are the earliest in French excepting only the isolated use in 1728 of *Cap a la Mort.* The brief attachment of the name *Abert Passage* to the strait appeared in 1842 on a chart of the *Survey of the Southern Entrance of Green Bay,* drawn by a lieutenant Simpson of the U. S. Topographical Engineers. The mystery is dispelled when we learn that a colonel in the same Engineers was one J. J. Abert. Three years later the Topographical Bureau's chart showed *Porte des Morts* passage. (Michigan exhibits 97, 98, 99 in *MichBrief.*)

84. *MichBrief,* 35-36.

85. The Sault Sainte Marie response (to writer, May 11, 1967), came from Librarian Sister Alice of Loretto Convent, who queried Fr. Robert Prud'homme, who in turn searched the longhand Ojibway and Chippewa dictionaries of Fr. Gagnier, S.J., and Bishop Baraga. The Newberry Library help came from Matt. P. Lowman, II (to writer, May 31, 1967). Personal letter, June 19, 1967. Problems inherent in this type of search may be inferred from the title of an 1873 booklet by James Hammond Trumbull: *Notes on Forty Algonkin Versions of the Lord's Prayer.*

86. Emma Helen Blair, translator and editor, *The Indian Tribes of the Upper Mississippi Valley,* etc., (Cleveland, 1911), I: 40-41n.

87. In L. P. Kellogg, *Early Narratives,* 338.

88. For example, Jared Sparks' *Life of Robert Cavelier de la Salle* (Boston, 1844), and Francis Parkman's *La Salle and the Discovery of the Great West* (Boston, 1884).

89. Hennepin, *A New Discovery,* 122.

90. In Blair, *The Indian Tribes.*

91. Indeed, the index to the magnificent sweep of our early history contained in those seventy-three volumes shows hot one reference to the Death's Door name in any of its probable mutations. Nor do the indexes to the *Michigan Pioneer and Historical Collections,* the *Territorial Papers of the United States,* Kellogg's *French Regime,* or Thwaites' *Early Western Travels.* All references in the *Wisconsin Historical Collections* have been considered in preparing this booklet, as have a number of early maps.

92. For convenience, we link the names here as custom has established, ignoring the suggestion of scholars like Grace Lee Nute (in *Caesars of the Wilderness*) that only one of the brothers-in-law journeyed this way.

93. *Wisconsin: A Guide to the Badger State,* Compiled by the Writers' Program of the Works Progress Administration (New York, 1941), 311.

INDEX

(This index was compiled by Eelin
Eaton, the author's wife.)

ABOUT THE ILLUSTRATOR

KATIE WEST received her B.F.A. from the Rhode Island School of Design and has been a professional artist for over 20 years. Currently she is employed by the National Institutes of Health as a graphic artist. Despite having lived in the Washington, D. C. area for almost 30 years, she is a Wisconsin girl in her heart. She was born in Sheboygan and grew up spending her summers on Washington Island. Both sides of her family have owned homes on the Island and been summer people since the early 1900's. Several relatives are living on or near the Island so her ties to the area are strong. The charms of the Island continue to draw her back to visit each summer.

Green Bay

PORTE DES MORTS PASSAGE

Plum Islan

Deathdoor Bluff

Table Bluff

Northport Pier →